A. de V. (Adelaide de Vendel) Chaudron

The First Reader

Designed for the Use of Primary Schools

A. de V. (Adelaide de Vendel) Chaudron

The First Reader
Designed for the Use of Primary Schools

ISBN/EAN: 9783744646499

Printed in Europe, USA, Canada, Australia, Japan

Cover: Foto ©Paul-Georg Meister /pixelio.de

More available books at **www.hansebooks.com**

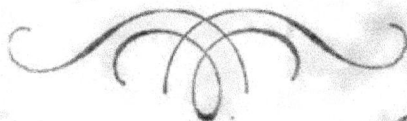

CHAUDRON'S SERIES.

THE

FIRST READER,

DESIGNED

FOR THE USE OF PRIMARY SCHOOLS.

SECOND EDITION.

Adopted for use in the Public Schools of Mobile.

By A. De V. CHAUDRON.

MOBILE, ALA.:

W. G. CLARK & CO., PUBLISHERS.

1864.

ADVERTISER AND REGISTER STEAM POWER PRESS.

PUBLISHERS' NOTICE.

———

The School Readers, of which this little book is the first number, have been prepared with much care and are specially adapted to the wants of our Southern Schools. They take the pupil at the threshold of his reading course and lead him gradually, step by step, along the way, making every thing plain before him, until he becomes a well-instructed and accomplished reader.

The author has patiently, zealously, laboriously, with a noble spirit of devotion and a rare appreciation of its requirements, brought her task nearly to completion. In addition to the best works in our own language, she has had at command a choice library of juvenile books in French and German, of which she has made good use. The translations to be found in this series are among the most attractive features of the READERS.

We are happy to be the medium of introducing these books to the public, and we regret that the restrictions of the blockade and the innumerable difficulties of publication in these times, forbid their appearance in a style equal to their merit. We prefer to publish them without pictorial embellishments other than a simple frontispiece: first, because the expense would so greatly enhance the cost of the books as to place them beyond the reach of the general public; and secodly, because it would be exceedingly difficult now to procure illustrations worthy of the name. When the war is over it will be easy to obtain suitable cuts in stereotype plates from abroad, when a new edition will be published supplying all present omissions.

Mobile, October, 1863.

Publishers' Notice to Second Edition.

THE demand for this series of Readers is almost unexampled, and assures them of a complete success. The original edition of the FIRST READER has been exhausted without filling the orders on hand, and it is now certain that a Second Edition of the SECOND READER will be required at an early day. The THIRD READER has been delayed by the non-receipt of the paper designed for it, but will soon be ready, and the FOURTH READER will speedily follow. In the present Edition of the FIRST READER, some typographical and other errors, which escaped correction in the first Edition, have been corrected, and the work generally revised. We trust that the time is not far distant when we can present this series of Readers with suitable illustrations and in the best style of such publications, making them in all respects worthy of the high rank they are destined to hold among the School Books of the South.

MOBILE, June 1st, 1864.

PREFACE.

THE plan of this little book is borrowed from the Ollendorf system of teaching languages, and it carries the child almost imperceptibly through its alphabetic difficulties.

From the first lesson in three letters to the last page of the book, the pupil is required to prepare but six new words in each new lesson.

The plurals of nouns already learned, form special and separate lessons.

After the words of five letters, those of two syllables follow, for the obvious reason that they are easier to learn than monosyllabic words of six letters.

No didactic teaching has been attempted. The lessons consist of short sentences on pleasant and familiar subjects.— It is hoped that they will be attractive to the little ones for whom they are written, and so will lighten the hours of their earliest school days.

No capital letters will be introduced before the 24th lesson. They are readily learned by a child who has mastered the smaller, but more important alphabet.

The Numerals also, may be taught, as they occur, at the beginning of each lesson.

A few rules lie at the foundation of all good Reading.

1st. Exact of children that they give its proper sound to each vowel. Above all, to the unaccented vowels *a*, *e*, and *o*.

2d. Teach them the correct sound of the long *u*.

EXAMPLES:

variety, (not varriutty;)   society, (not susshutty;

difficult, (not diffucult;)   resentment, (not ruzentmunt;)

revolution, (not revullootion.)

3d. Let them distinctly ring the *ing*.

EXAMPLES:

doing, (not doin ;)   pudding, (not puddin ;)

running, (not runnin ;)   &c.

4th. Last and most difficult of all to enunciate, without exaggeration, is the letter *r*.

1st. As heard in unaccented finals, as :

letter, (not lettuh ;)   mother, (not mothuh ;)

never, (not nevuh ;)   water, (not watuh ;)

2d. As sounded before a consonant, as :

horse, (not hoss:)   storm, (not staum ;) arm, (not awm.)

These rules cannot be learned by very young children, but the same children may be taught to observe any rule, by habit. The teacher who is willing to begin in the Primary Department itself, the philological reformation proposed in this course of Readers, will render incalculable service to the cause of education.

One step towards improvement in the elegant accomplishment of Reading might be taken, if in our public schools one teacher were appointed to give instructions to ALL classes in this particular branch. He should be one whose voice is well-modulated, and whose language is not only select in expression, but accurate in pronunciation and accent. Let him feel the importance of his calling as master of the Southern orators "to be ;" let him aspire to train the vocal organs of his pupils to their highest degree of lingual perfection, and he will have led them one step forward into the regions of Art. For Reading is an Art, scarcely subordinate to that of Music. The teachers of elocution, in our public schools, should be chosen as custodians of the purity of that magnificent language which has vibrated to the inspired touch of Milton's genius, and which Shakspeare has ennobled beyond any praise of ours.

A. V. C.

MOBILE, November 18th, 1862.

ALPHABET.

A B C D E

F G H I J

K L M N O

P Q R S T

U V W X Y

Z &

NUMERALS.

1 2 3 4 5 6 7 8 9 0

SMALL ALPHABET.

a b c d e f
g h i j k l m
n o p q r s t
u v w x y z

a b c d e f g h i j k l m
n o p q r s t u v w x y z

Exercises on the Alphabet.

a e i o u w y t l m p z k x

l n r v s d b h q g c j

o i t h p l m z s t k a u e l

v b e d t m q d l t e o f g s

l r m u c p d q

l m o b d e k z t i n p q

y h x v u n k l m o e d

l o i m r s b v o t r e a

m i œ æ fi fl ffi ffl &

t d b k h l j y g z q p

FIRST READER.

PART FIRST.

1st LESSON.

WORDS OF ONE LETTER.

I.	A.	O.

2d LESSON.

WORDS OF TWO LETTERS.

my	at	ox
us	by	is
me	of	ho
it	he	am

3d LESSON.

my ox.	it is he.
at us.	is it I?
by me.	am I he?
of it.	at my ox.

4th LESSON.

to	in	be
an	go	on
no	or	so
as	up	do

5th LESSON.

am I to go?	do I go?
I am to go.	it is an ox.
is he to go?	it is by me.
he is to go.	do as I do.

6th LESSON.

if	ax	my	on	we	of
an	as	be	am	my	no

7th LESSON.

if it be so.	he is to go up.
is it my ox?	am I up? no.
it is my ox.	he is up, so am I.
do I go?	he or I am up.

8th LESSON.

at	ox	if	us	he	be
ax	of	up	by	it	no

9th LESSON.

am I to go in?	he is in it.
go in, do.	go up as we do.
it is my ox.	do go on it as I do.
is he on it?	is it he or I?
is it by me?	is it my ax?

10th LESSON.

in	by	go	me	if	be
or	as	at	ox	to	us

11th LESSON.

is it so?	it is my ox.
it is so, by me.	it is no ox.
do as we do.	it is my ax.
if I go, do go by me.	is he up, or am I up?

12th LESSON.

*Lesson on some words formed by pre-fixing one
letter to words already learned.*

an	at	am	in	it
c-an	b-at	d-am	b-in	b-it
f-an	c-at	h-am	d-in	f-it
m-an	f-at	r-am	k-in	l-it
p-an	h-at	s-am	g-in	k-it
t-an	m-at	y-am	t-in	m-it
r-an	s-at		p-in	s-it

or	ox	up
f-or	b-ox	c-up
n-or	f-ox	p-up

13th LESSON.

Words of three letters.

hot	ten	pun	pad	keg
pot	men	nun	lad	leg
rot	den	fun	sad	beg
cot	wen	dun	mad	peg
lot	pen	sun	bad	bag

14th LESSON.

big	but	fop	mat	cup
dig	rut	top	bat	pup
fig	cut	hop	sat	tax
gig	hut	mop	fat	wax
jig	nut	pop	rat	vex

15th LESSON.

cat. fat. see. his. bad. the.

the cat.	see my fat cat.
my fat cat.	is it his cat?
see my cat.	is it his ox?
it is his cat.	is it my cat?
it is a bad cat.	see the bad ox.

16th LESSON.

the bad cat.	see my fat ox.
my bad cat.	a fat cat.
it is his fat ox.	it is his ax.
it is my bad ax.	is it my ox?
it is his bad cat.	it is my ox.

17th LESSON.

boy.   and.   too.   run.   pig.   can.

a boy and a fat ox.
a pig can run.
no, he is too fat to run.
the boy can run too.
so can the cat and the pig.
see my fat ox run.

18th LESSON.

the boy can run.	the cat and the boy.
is he a bad boy?	see my bad pig.
the pig and the ox.	the cat can run.
the boy is so fat.	and the ox too.
is the pig fat too?	no, the ox is too fat to run.
the ox is bad.	is the pig too fat?

19th LESSON.

The double s.

now.   puss.   not.   bit.   dog.   but.

the dog bit the boy.	puss can run too.
but not my dog.	puss is not fat.
my dog is not bad.	but the pig is too
his dog is bad.	fat to run.
and his pig too.	the dog bit puss.
the dog bit the ox.	he is a bad dog
his dog can run.	now.

20th LESSON.

big.   has.   cap.   top.   mug.   new.

the boy has a big top.

and a new cap too.

he has a mug.

his top is too big.

but not his mug.

it is my top and my cap.

I see a big cat.

I see a a fat pig.

and a bad dog too.

the boy has a new cap.

21st LESSON.

The double l.

hen.   let.   gun.   you.   get.   will.

will you get my new let me see the hen
    gun?   and the cat.
my big new gun.   the boy has my mug.
the hen is fat and the but not my fat hen.
    pig too.   get me my new top.
see the dog and the I see my big gun.
    pig.   do you see it too?
do you see the bee on no, I do not see the
    the mug?   gun.

22d LESSON.

saw   cup.   hat.   bee.   mud.   jug.

I saw a big bad dog. the jug is too big.
do you see my new the bee is on the
    cup?   cup.
the boy has on a now the cup is in the
    new hat.   mud.
I see a bee in my puss has my top.
    mug.   but the dog has it
my new cap is in the   not.
    mud.   I saw the bee and
do get the jug.   the hen.

23d LESSON.

cow. pen. pet. fly. rug. hum.

see my cow in the pen.
my big fat cow.
my bad pig is in the pen.
the cat bit you on the rug.
the bee can hum and fly.
my bad cat bit me.
see the dog and the cat on the rug.
the dog bit the big cow.
I see my fat pet hen.
the boy has on his new cap.
he has a gun and a top.
and a pig and an ox too.

24th LESSON.

With capital letters, but with no new words.

I see my pet cat, and the big boy has a
new hat.
See puss on the rug by me, and the fat
pig in the pen.
The dog bit the boy. The boy is so fat,
he can not run.
He has a new mug, a big top and a cup
for me.
Puss is on the mat ; will you get on the
mat too?
The bee can fly and hum, but the ox can
not.

My gun is new.   My top is red.   My hen
    is so fat.

I see the jug and the cup, the top and
    the mat.

The fat pig is in the mud, and the big
    cow is in the pen.

25th LESSON.

pin	six	bar	map	did
sin	fix	tar	sap	lid
win	mix	far	lap	hid
tin	pix	car	pap	bid
kin	ham	mar	nap	kid

26th LESSON.

try	pet	pan	cow	bit
dry	let	ran	saw	sit
fry	set	can	law	mit
sky	net	fan	daw	fit
sly	wet	tan	paw	lit

27th LESSON.

she.   for.   her.   had.   red.   rat.

The cat saw a rat on the rug, and she bit
    the rat.

The rat can run, but sly puss will see her.

I had a red top and a big gun. It was
not a bad gun.
My new cap is too big for me, and my
top will not hum.
Is his hen fat? No, she is not fat.

28th LESSON.

bed.   set.   sun.   yet.   sky.   sow.

See the sun how red it is! The sun has
not yet set.
The sky is red, the sun has set, and now
I will go to bed.
The cat is on my bed, and the dog is on
the rug.
He has an ox, a fat sow, a cow and a hen.
I saw a fly on my hat, and a bee in my
cup.

29th LESSON.

old.   fox.   man.   fill.   hay.   eat.

I see an old man, but he can not see me.
Do fill my new mug for puss and me.
The big red cow will eat up the new hay.
See the fat pig on the hay, by the cow
in the pen.
The sly fox will eat up my fat old hen.

30th LESSON.

lap.   one.   far.   sit.   out.   day.

I let my pet cat sit in my lap on the rug.

I can run as far as you, and so can my big dog.

I see a fox in the hen-pen, she can not get out.

One day the dog saw a fat sow, and he bit her.

The bee can fly, but the cow and the ox can not.

31st LESSON.

yes.   tea.   put.   hot.   pin.   tin.

The sun has set. May I go to bed now?

Yes, and I will get you a cup of hot tea.

Put it in my new tin cup for me, if it is too hot.

Can puss get a cup of hot tea too?

No, but puss can sit on the mat by the bed.

Now get me a pin to pin my cap, I will go to bed.

32d LESSON.

nut. log. cut. hop. use. log.

See my ax, it can cut a big log.

A saw can saw a big log too.

Let me see if you can use a saw.

Let me see if you can hop on one leg.

Will you eat a nut if I go and get you
  one?

33d LESSON.

box. ask. key. Ann. wet bag.

Do you see my box? It has a key to it.

Get my bag for me, and put it in the box.

I saw a boy by the hen-pen, hop on one
  leg.

Ask Ann if she saw my top on the rug.

Do get my pen, it is in the old tin box
  on the bed.

PART SECOND.

WORDS OF FOUR LETTERS.

34th LESSON.

Plural of words already learned.

In part Second, words of three letters will sometimes be introduced in the reading lessons without preparation.

The tops will not hum.
The hens and bees can fly.
But the dogs and cows can not.
I see the fat pigs in the pen.
You saw the rats run and the cats too.
Will you get the cups and mugs?
Bad boys will run out in the mud.
I see the rugs and the new caps.
The mats are by the beds.
I saw my keys and pens in the tin box.
Get the guns and the dogs and we
     will go.
The men saw the bags on the bed.
The jugs are on the mat.

35th LESSON.

sake	cave	gold	line	dray
rake	save	told	nine	clay
wake	pave	bold	pine	stay
lake	wave	sold	fine	play
take	nave	cold	mine	pray

36th LESSON.

Pronounce the R.		Pronounce the R.				
	cart		dark	heat	veal	must
	tart		bark	meat	meal	dust
	hart		lark	seat	heal	rust
	part		park	beat	seal	gust
	dart		mark	neat	teal	just

37th LESSON.

with.   room.   must.   ball.   tree.   find.

I can cut a tree with my new ax.

But you must go and find the ax for
     me.

Will you go out and get my big ball?

I must go in the room to see if Puss
     is on the bed.

Oh no; Puss is not in the room, she
     is by the tree.

38th LESSON.

milk.   good.   some.   like.   have.   much.

Do fill my mug with some new milk.
Milk is good. I like it so much.
A good boy will go to bed if he is
    told to go.
Yes, but may he not have his tea?
Oh yes, he must have his tea and
    some milk too.

39th LESSON.

your.   nice.   hang.   wall.   give.   cake.

I will give you some milk and some
    nice cake.
Do you like cake and milk? Oh yes,
    I do.
Do you see my new gun hang on the
    wall?
Yes, do give it to me. It is too big
    for you.
Now, you must go to bed, and so must
    Puss.

40th LESSON.

fire. take. make. poor. rich. cold.

Puss is cold. Do take her on your lap, by the fire.

Poor puss! Are you cold? If you are, come in my lap.

Puss can run up a tree, but she can not fly like a bee.

I have a good dog and a nice cow.

Make your cow give me a cup of rich milk.

41st LESSON.

love. hunt. warm. roll. play. when.

I love to sit by a warm fire when I am cold.

I like to see puss play on the rug and roll my ball.

You have a good gun, and a fine dog too.

Do you hunt with your dog and your gun?

No, but I can play ball and hum tops.

2

42d LESSON.

spin.   what.   **name.**   **Dash.**   foot.   then.

You can play foot-ball with me, and
    then we can spin tops.

Oh, what a fine foot-ball! It is so big!

Has our dog a name? Yes, his name
    is Dash.

Is Dash a good name for a dog?

Yes, it is a fine name.

I have a cat, and her name is Pet.

43d LESSON.

yard.   come.   pond.   eggs.   swim.   laid.

Come in the yard, and play with me.

Let us play by the pond and see Dash
    swim.

Have the hens laid some eggs to-day?

Oh yes! See what a nice new-laid
    egg I have.

Now let us go and play foot-ball in
    the yard.

44th LESSON.

lamb.　keep.　bird.　cage.　Dick.　four.

I have a lamb, and I keep it in the yard.

A lamb, a bird, a dog and a cat. Four pets.

My lamb will play in the yard with you.

I have a bird, too, and I keep it in a cage.

Have you a name for your bird?

Yes, his name is Dick.

45th LESSON.

doll.　stay.　here.　babe,　does.　why.

I keep my bird in my room.

He does not stay in a tree.

Here is my new doll; she can cry like a babe.

I have a doll, too, but she is not new.

I like to play with my doll, and make her cry.

Poor doll! Why do you like to make her cry?

46th LESSON.

hurt.   girl.   feel.   Rose.   mine.   crib.

It does not hurt her to cry, she can not feel.

My doll has a bed. And mine has a crib.

Here is Puss. Come, Puss, and play doll with Rose and me.

Why, Puss can not play dolls, but I will tell you what she can do.

She can play ball, and eat up a bird or a rat.

47th LESSON.

drum.   beat.   John.   down.   duck.   fife.

John has a drum, and I can beat on it.

John beats his drum by the tree in the yard.

I love to hear the drum beat, and the fife play.

I fell down to-day and hurt my foot.

I hurt my foot by the pond, that is for the ducks.

48th LESSON.

take.   ripe.   figs.   nest.   feed.   well.

Do give me some cake to feed my
    bird.

Does your bird eat cake? Oh yes,
    and ripe figs and eggs too.

Well, take some cake to your bird, and
    here is some for you.

My fat hen has laid a new egg in her
    nest to-day.

My hen has a nest in the yard by the
    well.

49th LESSON.

lame.   dime.   from.   hand.   wine.   knee.

See that poor boy in the yard. He
    is lame.

How did he get lame? He fell from
    a tree.

One day he fell down and hurt his
    knee.

Poor boy! Let us give him some cake
    and wine.

Give him some cake, and put a dime
    in his hand.

50th LESSON.

glad. home. ride. soon. town. time.

The boy was glad to get the dime.
  He will take it home.
Now you and I must put on our hats,
  and go to town.
If we do not go soon, we will not be
  home in time for tea.
If I am a good girl to-day, will you
  let me take a ride too?
I like to ride, and I like to run in the
  yard and play.

51st LESSON.

talk. blue. come. eyes. down. pail.

Come, let us take the pail, and go to
  the well,
And get some wood to make a nice,
  warm fire.
No, let us sit down by the fire, and
  talk.
Let me see your doll. She has blue
  eyes.
We must take your doll with us to
  ride to town.

52d LESSON.

cook.   tell.   bake.   that.   corn.   pick.

Come, let us go and feed the hens with
    some corn.

See how the hens pick up the corn and
    eat it !

Hens love to pick up corn, and cows like
    to eat hay.

Now tell the cook to get some eggs, and
    bake us a cake.

Do you like cake? Yes, I like cake, and
    so does John.

53d LESSON.

read.   gave.   this.   look.   book.   goat.

Can this boy read? Yes, he can read
    in this book.

Who gave him this nice, new book to
    read?

I gave it to him, and I will give one to
    you too.

But you must be good, and do all that I
    tell you to do.

Look at the goat pick up hay in the yard.

The goat and the cow love hay, and the
    hens love corn.

54th LESSON.

colt. torn. mare. whip. gate. best.

Do you see the mare and her colt by the
  gate?

Do you like the colt or the mare best?
  Oh, I like the colt best.

See how Puss has torn my new book.
  Bad Puss!

Let us whip her then. Oh no, do not
  hurt poor Puss.

She will be good, and I will give her
  some nice milk,

And we will go to play in the yard, and
  see the colt run.

55th LESSON.

deer. wait. stay. next. find. see.

May I go with Dick and Dash to hunt
  deer to-day?

No, you must wait for a time yet, you
  are not a man.

Stay at home with me, and read your
  new book.

My book is not here, I will go and find
  it.

Your book is on the bed in the next
  room.

Take a seat now, and read for Rose and
  me.

56th LESSON.

sail.　high.　kite.　done.　wind.　when.

If I have time to-day, I will sail my new kite.

The wind is so high that she will sail well.

And when I have done, I will ride on the mare.

The mare and her colt are in town with John.

Then I can not ride, and I must wait.

Will you get a whip for me when I ride?

57th LESSON.

shut.　they.　door.　feet　them.　jump.

Shut the door, it is cold in this room.

Do you feel cold? Yes, my feet are cold.

Are they? Then come and warm them by the fire.

Look in the yard, and see the colt how it runs.

And the lamb too. Oh, do let me go and play with them!

Well, go jump and run, and you will get warm.

58th LESSON.

coat.　tear.　rope.　cart.　fast.　draw.

You must take your coat, or you will
　take cold.

Now run as fast as you can, but do not
　tear your coat.

Can you run as fast as a deer or a colt?

No, but I love to jump with them on a
　cold day.

I feel so warm when I jump the rope.

Now I will put my goat to a cart, and he
　will draw Puss.

Puss will be glad to ride in a cart.

59th LESSON.

till	dawn	moon	lane	kind
mill	yawn	boon	cane	find
kill	pawn	soon	mane	mind
bill	fawn	coon	sane	bind
will	lawn	noon	pane	rind

60th LESSON.

Pronounce the E.

sore	face	bone	mice	male
more	lace	hone	nice	pale
core	mace	lone	rice	sale
bore	race	zone	vice	tale
wore	pace	tone	dice	bale

61st LESSON.

A few simple words of two syllables.

ta-per. po-ker. ba-by. park. burn. wa-fer.

When I was in the park to-day, I saw a poor ba-by.

The ba-by was so cold, that I took it home to warm it.

I gave it a cup of milk and a nice wa-fer to eat.

Do you burn a ta-per or a lamp in your room?

Will you be so good as to stir the fire with a po-ker?

The po-ker is not here, it is in the next room.

62d LESSON.

un-tie. ci-gar. ci-der. a-pron. shoe. la-zy.

Can you un-tie your shoe? No, I can not un-tie it.

Give the old man a ci-gar and a mug of ci-der.

Will you hang my a-pron for me by the fire to dry?

Your a-pron is now dry, and you may put it on.

I do not wish to put it on, I wish to give it to that poor girl.

She is a la-zy girl; you must not give her your nice a-pron.

63d LESSON.

li-on. man-y. an-y. a-way. No-ra. year.

I have been to a show, and I saw a big
  li-on in a cage.

What a good fire No-ra has made in our
  room for us.

I was cold at the show, but I am not cold
  an-y more.

Tom has gone to sea ; he is in the na-vy.

He will be a-way from home for one long
  year.

No-ra did not find an-y eggs to-day in
  her grey hen's nest.

64th LESSON.

bi-ble. an-ger. pa-pa. Cla-ra. cra-zy. bless.

Pa-pa says that if we give way to an-ger,
  God will not bless us.

He says, too, that we must be good to
  the poor, and help them ;

And that we must not make fun of poor
  cra-zy Cla-ra.

John gave her a pair of shoes the last
  time she came here.

John is a good boy ; he can read his bi-ble,

And God will bless him, if he is kind to
  cra-zy Cla-ra.

PART THIRD.

WORDS OF FIVE LETTERS.

In part Third, words of less than five letters will be sometimes introduced without preparation.

65th LESSON.

Words already learned, with the s added to them.

I like to see new-laid eggs in the hens' nests.

John loves guns and dogs, and I love dolls and cats.

Boys like to sail kites and to hunt birds.

Girls, as well as boys, love to ride and to roll balls.

Come, let us go to feed the pigs and the colts.

When the sun sets the skies look like gold.

Anne gave me some nice cakes to-day.

John cut two pine trees in the woods with an ax.

I sold my ducks for nine dimes to Dick.

The cows and goats have come home to their pens.

The carts and the whips are in the yard.

66th LESSON.

shall. chair. large. grass. boat. thing.

John shall have a large kite, and sail it
in the yard.

And what may I have? You shall have
some-thing too.

It shall be a fine chair for your doll to
sit in,

And a boat to sail in the pond in the yard.

Come, let us sit on the grass by this large
tree.

May I roll on the grass and play with
Dash?

67th LESSON.

house. Frank. lunch. catch. bread. piece.

Let us go in the house and get some-thing
to eat.

It is lunch-time. I will take some bread
and milk.

And Frank will have bread and meat for
his lunch.

Rose will like to have a piece of that
large cake.

See how Puss jumps to beg for bread and
meat.

Puss sees a bird in that large tree. She
likes to catch birds.

It is time to go in the house. It is too
warm in the sun.

68th LESSON.

grate. floor. black. clean. swept. coal.

Has Ann made a good fire in the grate?

Yes, and she swept the floor clean.

Well, then, let us sit by the fire to warm
our feet.

See how red the fire is! And yet it is
made of black coal.

When coal is cold it is black, but when
it is hot it is red.

You may take my chair and sit by the
warm grate.

I have been in the yard, and I am not cold.

69th LESSON.

shoes. quite. hands. while. where. light.

Rose, come in the house, or you will
catch cold.

Jane, let me see if your hands are clean.

No, they are quite black, and your shoes
are wet.

Where have you been? By the pond in
the yard.

Sit on this chair, and dry your feet by
the fire.

What a large fire we have in the grate!
Who made it?

Ann made it while you were out at play.

Now it is quite dark, we must have a light.

70th LESSON.

drive. bring. horse. green. small. think.

Frank, can you drive a horse and a cart?

Not yet, but I can sail a small boat and
a large kite.

John can drive a horse and dray to town.

But John is a man, and he can do what
I can not.

I have a small dog-cart, and Dash and I
bring wood in it.

A bird has made her nest in the tall grass
in the woods.

Let us go and see it. It is full of small
green eggs.

I do not think the eggs are green, I think
they are blue.

71st LESSON.

climb. flock. fence. sheep. touch. drove.

Do you like to climb trees and see the
birds' nests.

Yes; but I do not touch the birds, I look
at the eggs.

Rose can climb a fence, but she can not
climb a tree.

She saw a large flock of sheep come in
the yard to-day.

The dogs ran at the sheep, and drove
them in the pen.

The ducks, the goats, and the cows all
ran too.

Dick drove our large black horse to town
to-day.

Do you think he will bring us some-thing
nice from town?

72d LESSON.

which. shelf. place. spoil. leave. none.

John, which book shall I bring you
to read now?

Bring me the green book from the
book-shelf.

I do not see your green book. Where
is it?

When I left the house, I put it on the
chair.

A chair is no place on which to leave
books.

If you spoil your books, you will have
none to read.

And if Anne spoils her dolls, she will
have none to play with.

73d LESSON.

crush	taste	blank	grain	slate
brush	waste	flank	brain	plate
flush	haste	thank	chain	grate
blush	baste	drank	train	state
plush	paste	crank	drain	crate

74th LESSON.

crave	shock	brown	swine	stick
brave	crock	frown	thine	brick
slave	frock	drown	brine	quick
grave	clock	crown	twine	thick
shave	block	clown	shine	trick

75th LESSON.

storm. night. cloud. clear. fruit. grow.

I see a black cloud in the sky. We will
have a storm.

Shut the door to keep out the rain and
the cold.

Rain will make the trees and the fruit
grow.

Will rain make Puss grow? No, but it
will make figs grow.

I like to hear it rain at night when I am
in bed.

But in the day-light, I love to see the sun
shine.

Now the sky is black no more, it is quite
clear.

76th LESSON.

there. world. brown. seems. sweet. James.

There is Rose ; she has on a dark brown
  cloak.
Rose has a sweet face ; she is a good girl.
So is Bell. Bell has large black eyes,
And they seem to laugh when she looks
    at you.
And Anne, with her sweet grey eyes,
    seems to love all the world.
If we are kind and good, all the world
    will love us.
James is a good boy, and at home we all
    love him.

77th LESSON.

horse. proud. field. white. throw. break.

I like to see a fine horse run in a field.
He likes to kick up his heels, and throw
    back his head,
And he looks so proud and so glad and free.
My horse is a brown bay with a black
    mane.
And mine is white, and I call him Snow-
    drop.
I love to catch him in the field and ride
    him.
I saw a horse break a cart to-day.

78th LESSON.

blame	grist	make
frame	twist	flake
shame	whist	brake
flame	whisk	shake
sperm	brisk	quake

Pronounce the R.

thorn	pound
shorn	found
store	sound
shore	bound
snore	round

79th LESSON.

trick	steam	might
brick	cream	fight
quick	dream	sight
prick	bream	right
stick	gleam	night

crash	chink
gnash	drink
flash	brink
trash	clink
clash	slink

PART FOURTH.

80th LESSON.

WORDS OF FIVE LETTERS WITH THE ADDITION OF S.

The grates are clean, and the floors are swept.

The chairs are in the house in the rooms.

The lights are out, and the place is dark.

The clouds are black, and it will soon rain.

The warm cloaks are on the shelf in my room.

I saw two droves of sheep on the road to-day.

I think that cakes and figs are nice things to eat.

PART FIFTH.

81st LESSON.

SIMPLE WORDS OF TWO SYLLABLES AND OF SIX LETTERS.

Ma-ry.	ma-ma.	bas-ket.
wa-ter.	su-gar.	ver-y.

Ma-ry has a nice bas-ket to hold her work.

Ma-ry can put her doll and mine in her bas-ket.

Give me some su-gar, ma-ma, to put in my tea.

Rose has a small bas-ket made all of su-gar.

Of su-gar? Then her bas-ket must be good to eat.

John, do you like to sail in a boat on the wa-ter?

Oh yes, John has been to sail and he likes it very much.

82d LESSON.

ta-ble. ap-ple. hun-gry. bis-cuit. but-ter. man-y.

Jane, set the ta-ble, for we are hun-gry.

And bring us some bread, and some wa-
ter to drink.

Will you have some fresh but-ter with
your bread?

And an apple too? I have some in my
bas-ket.

Oh yes, and a bis-cuit too, if you will
give us one.

So you will have an ap-ple, a bis-cuit,
some bread and but-ter.

How ver-y good you are, Ma-ma, to give
us so man-y things.

Do you think so? Then you must be
ver-y good to Ma-ma too.

83d LESSON.

cof-fee. po-ny. les-son. school. pret-ty. din-ner.

I like my cof-fee ver-y sweet, will you
give me some more su-gar?

Yes, my dear, and then you must go and
learn your les-son.

You have a ver-y pret-ty book to learn
your les-son in.

See what a pret-ty po-ny Frank rides
down the lane.

Where has Frank been to-day? He has
    been to school.
And when school is out, he goes home to
    get his din-ner.
Well, I think it quite nice to ride from
    school on a po-ny.

84th LESSON.

sto-ry. lit-tle. ba-ker. af-ter. sup-per. mar-ble.

James, come to me, my dear, and I will
    tell you a pret-ty sto-ry.
And then you shall go to the ba-ker, and
    get some bread.
May I get some cake and rusk for our
    sup-per, Ma-ma?
Yes, but do not stay long; lit-tle boys
    must not be out af-ter dark.
May I bring lit-tle Dick home to take
    sup-per with us?
Yes, and you may take some fresh but-ter
    to the lame boy.
Poor boy! I will stay a lit-tle while and
    play mar-bles with him.

85th LESSON.

Em-ma. ev-er cot-ton. ne-gro. plan-ter. Dix-ie

Em-ma, have you ev-er been in a large
    cot-ton field?

Oh yes, and the cot-ton bolls looks as white as snow.

The cot-ton plan-ter lives on-ly in the South.

Did you ev-er hear the ne-gro men sing Dix-ie?

Oh yes, and I have seen them pick cot-ton too.

They have a large bas-ket to put the cot-ton in.

Cot-ton is as pret-ty as snow, but it is worth a great deal more.

80th LESSON.

bet-ter. in-to. sis-ter. ba-sin. un-til. cous-in.

In the South we make cot-ton, su-gar, rice and cof-fee.

And we make corn, too, for in the South we like corn bread.

Em-ma likes corn bread bet-ter than she does ba-ker's bread.

Stay here, James, by your lit-tle sis-ter, un-til I come back.

I must go into the house, but I will be back in a lit-tle while.

I must fill this ba-sin with wa-ter to wash my hands.

Tell my lit-tle cous-in Ma-ry to come here and play with me.

87th LESSON.

so-fa. dol-lar. la-zy. bought. tired. can-dy.

Come, lit-tle Ann, and sit by me on this
    large so-fa.

Ann and Ma-ma feel very la-zy, and they
    want to rest.

We are not la-zy, Ma-ma ; we are tired
    with our long walk.

That is true, my dear ; to be la-zy and to
    be tired are not the same thing.

What did you buy with the dol-lar I gave
    you to-day?

I bought some can-dy for Rose, and a
    whip for Dick.

And I bought some cakes for the poor
    boy that is sick.

88th LESSON.

pan-cake. flow-er. spi-der. gru-el. la-dy. doc-tor.

Jane, tell the cook to make pan-cakes for
    din-ner.

I saw a large black spi-der on the wall
    to-day.

I met a la-dy in town with pret-ty black
    eyes.

She had a flow-er in her hand, and she
    gave it to me.

I put it in my bas-ket, and will take it
    home to sis-ter.

When lit-tle boys are sick, we feed them
　　on gru-el.

And we send for the doc-tor to make
　　them well.

89th LESSON.

	Pronounce the R.	
na-vy	pa-per	san-dy
ro-sy	ta-per	dan-dy
ho-ly	ca-per	han-dy
po-sy	sa-fer	ban-dy
co-sy	ra-zor	can-dy

	Pronounce the R.
pen-ny	cop-per
ben-ny	hop-per
sun-ny	prop-er
fun-ny	let-ter
ma-ny	set-ter

90th LESSON.

			Pronounce the R.
sor-ry	can-non	pock-et	o-ver
jol-ly	lin-en	dock-et	nev-er
fol-ly	cab-in	lock-et	riv-er
sal-ly	sat-in	rock-et	liv-er
hil-ly	lat-in	socket	giv-er
sil-ly	mat-in	jack-et	gun-ner

91st LESSON.

On some of the preceding words.

Rose is a han-dy girl, she has made her doll a sat-in dress.

A gun-ner is a man who fires off can-non.

I was in the cab-in of a boat on the riv-er.

I had not a pen-ny in my pock-et, and I was quite sor-ry.

I ne-ver saw such a jol-ly, fun-ny boy as Tom.

Give me a piece of pa-per, that I may write a let-ter.

The place was ver-y hilly, and the day was sun-ny.

You were ver-y sil-ly to give your lock-et for a ra-zor.

John wore a lin-en jack-et, and his setter was with him.

92d LESSON.

IRREGULAR PLURALS OF WORDS OF FIVE LETTERS ALREADY LEARNED.

Plurals of words of two syllables.

Did you see the hor-ses jump o-ver the fences?

I put the books on the shelves in their pla-ces.

Ann tells us ver-y pret-ty sto-ries when we know our les-sons.

The bis-cuits and ap-ples are all in the bas-kets.

The ta-bles in those hou-ses are all of mar-ble.

I will buy some dress-es and some flow-ers for my cous-ins.

My jack-ets are too large, and my ra-zors are dull.

I saw the rock-ets go up on a ver-y dark night.

Frank's pock-ets are full of mar-bles.

I paid ten pen-nies for my cous-in's let-ter.

93d LESSON.

nee-dle. cur-ly. thim-ble. bon-net. fin-ger. gar-den.

Ann can use her nee-dle to make a doll's
dress.

She has a thim-ble on her fin-ger, and her
nee-dle will not hurt it.

She has a work-box of rose-wood with a
lock and key.

Her doll has cur-ly hair, and she has a
pret-ty bon-net.

Ann's Ma-ma made the bon-net of blue
sat-in.

Em-ma's black hen has made a nest in
the gar-den.

The hor-ses have gone to the well to get
some wa-ter.

94th LESSON.

or-gan. or-ange. mon-key. can-not. mu-sic. giv-en.

Em-ma, come and see the mon-key in the
street.

She has on a short red dress, and a lit-tle
bon-net.

The man that leads her plays on the or-gan,

And the mon-key hops up and down to
the mu-sic.

Now throw the mon-key a piece of your
bis-cuit.

Ma-ry has just giv-en her a bit of or-ange.

And she can not take the bis-cuit just yet.

Aft-er a while, she will take it from you.

Script.

A *A* B *B* C *C* D *D*

E *E* F *F* G *G* H *H*

I *I* J *J* K *K* L *L*

M *M* N *N* O *O* P *P*

Q *Q* R *R* S *S* T *T*

U *U* V *V* W *W* X *X*

Y *Y* Z *Z*

a *a* b *b* c *c* d *d* e *e* f *f* g *g* h *h*

i *i* j *j* k *k* l *l* m *m* n *n* o *o* p *p* q *q*

r *r* s *s* t *t* u *u* v *v* w *w* x *x* y *y* z *z*

1st LESSON.

my	at	ox	to	in	if
as	by	is	an	go	an
me	of	am	no	or	ax
it	ho	he	as	up	me

2d LESSON.

my ox	it is he	I am to go
at us	is it I?	he is to go
by me	am I he?	am I to go?
of it	at my ox	is he to go?

3d LESSON.

The boy can run.

Is it a bad boy?

The pig and the ox.

The ox is bad.

The boy is so fat.

The ox is bad.

The cat and the boy.

See my bad pig.

The cat can run.

And the ox too.

No, the ox is too fat.

Is the pig too fat?

4th LESSON.

The dog bit the boy.
But not my dog.
My dog is not bad.
His dog is bad,
And his pig too.
The dog bit the ox.
This dog can run.
Puss can run too.
The ox is not fat.
The pig is too fat to run.
The dog bit Puss.
He is a bad dog now.

THE END.

www.ingramcontent.com/pod-product-compliance
Lightning Source LLC
Chambersburg PA
CBHW022035080426
42733CB00007B/845